AN OVERVIEW OF WORLD-MACRO

Protecting Your Balance Sheet at a Critical Time

Fernando Walter Lolo and Cathal Rabbitte

© 2017 Fernando Walter Lolo and Cathal Rabbitte
www.DirectionalAlpha.com

ALL RIGHTS RESERVED. This book contains material protected under International and Federal Copyright Laws and Treaties. Any unauthorized reprint or use of this material is prohibited. No part of this book may be reproduced or transmitted in any form or by any means, electronic or mechanical, including photocopying, recording, or by any information storage and retrieval system without express written permission from the authors/publisher.

Copyright © 2017 Authored by Fernando Walter Lolo and Cathal Rabbitte

All rights reserved.

CONTENTS

A SPECIAL NOTE TO OUR READERS I

ABOUT THE AUTHORS III

DEDICATION IX

ACKNOWLEDGEMENTS X

INTRODUCTION 1

WORLD-MACRO STATUS AS OF JULY 2017 4

DEBT LEVELS 13

BLIND SPOTS: BUSINESS-AS-USUAL (BAU) WHEN NOTHING IS AS PER USUAL 16

MARKET PSYCHOLOGY: MARK-TO-MARKET VERSUS MARK-TO-REALITY 20

IS THE TIME VALUE OF MONEY SUSPENDED? YIELD CURVES, INTEREST RATES POLICIES, SOLVENCY 2 25

WORLD POLARIZATION SNAPSHOT AS OF JULY 2017 29

IS BREXIT AN ECONOMIC OR A GEOPOLITICAL MOVE? 33

OIL PRICES IN A NUTSHELL 38

A QUESTION OF SPEED? 40

CONCLUSION 46

DISCLAIMER 48

A SPECIAL NOTE TO OUR READERS

Dear Colleague,

Thank you for claiming your copy of **"An Overview of World-Macro - Protecting Your Balance Sheet at a Critical Time."**

This book will **provide you** with critical **high-level insights on systemic risk, financial modeling, investment opportunities, balance sheet hedging, and fiduciary duty**, *different approaches, and more that every Investor, Chairman, Chief Executive Officer, Chief Investment Officer, Chief Risk Management Officer, Board Member needs today.*

AN OVERVIEW OF WORLD MACRO

Let's get started with providing high-level insight to detect **what is wrong at the system level in today's markets; detecting early warnings on systemic risk, volatility events, and markets uncertainties; to enable better decision making** *on balance sheet priority risk detection and response* right now…

Sincerely,

Fernando Walter Lolo and Cathal Rabbitte

www.DirectionalAlpha.com

ABOUT THE AUTHORS

Fernando Walter Lolo and Cathal Rabbitte specialize in systemic risk, financial modeling, investments, balance sheet hedging, and fiduciary duty at www.DirectionalAlpha.com whose accomplishments include:

Fernando Walter Lolo

- Fernando Walter Lolo specializes in Alternative Investments and Global-Macro strategies. Fernando founded Directional Alpha as a private asset management fund focused exclusively on tail risk, volatility trading, and hedging. In 2017, Directional Alpha was re-launched as a knowledge-driven boutique, with a relentless forward looking focus on systemic risk and world-macro conditions.
- Fernando has 20+ years of global track record in finance. Fernando focuses his businesses on solid ground unconventional/unorthodox approaches, as

part of a difficult built-up rethought process of traditional/conventional methods.

- Fernando focuses on volatility, tail risks, and world-macro financial events, and he was also an active angel investor only in high-impact selective deals. He has advised on international finance, FSB - Financial Stability Board, and G-20 high-profile related issues at the Ministry of Economy and Finance of Argentina. Prior to that, he worked in Global Alternative Investments for 10+ years at the World Bank Group in Washington, DC. Before that, he worked in Quantitative Finance, Corporate Finance, and Risk Management in Latin America (LATAM).

- Fernando refined his specializations at Ivy-leagues by focusing on Investments, Fundraising, Investor Psychology-Risk Profiles, Global-Macro & Prop Trading, and Geopolitical International Finance. Fernando holds an MBA, a Master in Finance, and Post-graduate Degrees in Financial Engineering & Quantitative Finance from Harvard University, Columbia University, Universidad Torcuato Di Tella, Universidad de Buenos Aires, and Johns Hopkins University. In addition, he is a Certified Public Accountant (Argentina) and holds the CAIA designation (Chartered Alternative Investment Analyst) from CAIA Association.

- During his career, Fernando worked in the US, Emerging Markets (LATAM), and Europe.

Cathal Rabbitte

- Cathal Rabbitte, FIA is an actuary, analyst, strategist, and journalist specializing in modeling coherence and the translation of developing macro economic themes into usable modeling insights and workable strategy.

- Cathal serves as external Contributing Editor at Directional Alpha. He has over 20 years of experience in Europe, Asia, and Africa, primarily in insurance and reinsurance.

- As a journalist, he has extensive archiving and research experience as well as broad and deep knowledge of historical trends with a strong ability to put risk into cultural and historical contexts and to help articulate the limits of financial modeling to detect signals of the future and to minimize risk given economic turbulence.

- Cathal has over 15 years of experience reporting and analyzing economic themes for various media. Cathal has analyzed and written extensively about corporate collapses and the near death of top global Reinsurance and Insurance Companies during the initial stage of the World Financial crisis in 2008-10. The key in those cases was incoherent modeling and poor corporate governance responses to shifting risk developments.

Work History:

- Before the 2008 crisis, both authors already foresaw that crisis coming while working at other

AN OVERVIEW OF WORLD MACRO

organizations (World Bank Group and Swiss Re). They were exposed to market crises such as the Mexican "Tequila" crisis, Asian "Tigers" crisis, Brazil, Ecuador, Argentina crisis, Russian crisis, the dot-com crisis, geopolitical crisis, tail events such as 2008 crisis, and other events of high volatility such as China markets volatility events, Brexit, the 2016 US Elections, French Elections, and alike.

- The authors have developed complementary skills by mastering traditional methods, and then subsequently unconventional methods in finance, world macro economics, investments, markets, volatility, tail, and systemic risks.

- The authors focus on world-macro strategies and specialize in coherent high-level analysis aiming to avoid the group think of the market. Even before re-launching Directional Alpha in 2017, the authors have re-confirmed that financial markets continue to be heavily influenced by group think. This reality calls for a fresh view incorporating the fact that markets are not in business-as-usual any longer, and therefore, modeling needs to reflect this in order to protect fiduciary duty.

- The high-level insights in this book are not driven by what the markets are doing. The authors do not follow market trends, but we consider a mosaic view of the system, including fundamentals, technical, history, asset bubbles, debt, geopolitics, international relations, power considerations and investment finance.

- This book's core focus is on systemic and tail risks which are ignored by markets and not reflected in market pricing. The authors look at structural reasons behind developments, and also why prior events happen. They understand the key difference between cyclical and systematic crises.

- They have strong communications skills and deep market knowledge concerning events over the last 30 years. Both authors understand many weaknesses in modeling and investments given that very few models take a systematic world approach as they do, as they instead mostly follow market pricing views. They are interested in what is happening and not in what people think is happening. After a long walk, they re-created Directional Alpha - World-Macro.

Personal Information:

- The authors come from different backgrounds, having complimentary skillsets, and a mix of insurance-macro and hedge fund global-macro investment skills.
- Given their worldwide experience, it was to be expected that we might have different views and angles about politics, current affairs, and so on; however, we believe that our diverse backgrounds and experience foster respect, integrity, humility, and further, to focus on discussing the best solutions to any topic by focusing on What is right, rather than Who of us is right. We consider this is one of our great Assets. Our focus is on risk and opportunity.
- Both authors have a solid experience over a wide range of geographies (US, EU, Latin America, Asia,

Middle East, and Eastern Europe). Their understanding of cultures, doing businesses, finance, investments, and politics across many languages is high level.

- They have extensive experience in world macro issues such as financial crises, tail risks, modeling weaknesses, G-20, Financial Stability Board - FSB issues, Insurance & Financial Regulations, Pensions, Hedge Funds, Asset Management, Alternative Investments, Regulations (e.g. Solvency 2, Basel III), Investment Management, Fundraising, Investor Psychology, Trading, Corporate Finance, Journalism, and Risk Management.

- In a nutshell, they have developed a thorough understanding of the underlying drivers of world macro events. As a result, we are driven to demystify often complex subjects into the form of accessible analytics, with a focus on coherent problem-solving approaches.

DEDICATION

To our Kids: Benjamin, Tim, and Éadaoin.

To our Families, Corinne, Friends, Colleagues, and Readers, past, present, and future.-

In memory of Jean Francois Perroud
And Jorge Walter Lolo.

ACKNOWLEDGEMENTS

Thanks to all who accompanied us on this long journey, which was a long Walk.

www.DirectionalAlpha.com

INTRODUCTION

This book addresses key fundamentals of **how World-Macro dynamics work in order to detect early warnings of systemic risks and financial crises**. It will provide you with **critical high-level insights** on Systemic Risk, Financial Modeling, Investment Opportunities, Balance Sheet Hedging, and Fiduciary Duty. It is designed *to examine the key elements of World-Macro risks* in the global economic system, **which is ignored by financial markets and conventional modeling**.

This book **focuses_on mapping the key areas of risk in the global economic system** that are ignored by financial markets and conventional modeling. **It is not good enough to rely on markets for a sense of security. It provides high-level insights** *every Investor, Chairman, Chief Executive Officer, Chief Investment Officer, Chief Risk Management Officer, Board Member* **needs to have to know what is happening at the system level in order to fulfill the fiduciary duty.**

AN OVERVIEW OF WORLD MACRO

The biggest risks are not in the data; therefore, mistakes happen. This book provides critical insights to help reduce those mistakes that most often cause **Investors, Chairmen, CEOs, CIOs, CROs, Board Members** to *fail completely* with these issues and **what information they need to AVOID!**

These mistakes stop most of them dead in their tracks, really before they ever even get started. In summary, this book provides:

- High-level insights on how to understand *World-Macro dynamics to detect early warnings of systemic risk formation and financial crises.*

- *It maps risks to detect what is wrong at the system level* in today's markets.

- Coherent assessments of *early warnings on systemic risk, volatility events, and markets uncertainties.*

- Solid analyses for better decision making on *balance sheet priority risk detection and response.*

- Assessments of *risks and opportunities beyond market groupthink to support suitable alternative hedges and reallocation* scenarios.

Fernando Walter Lolo and Cathal Rabbitte are well-known specialists on the subject of World-Macro and are sharing their experience to help People avoid the most damaging mistakes in this area; so every **Investor, Chairman, CEO, CIO, CRO, Board Member** can understand **how World-Macro dynamics work in order to**

detect early warnings of systemic risk and financial crises and to protect their balance sheets at a critical time.

So, let's just jump right in.

WORLD-MACRO STATUS AS OF JULY 2017

"*May 1989*

Jim: *Hello Mr. Mills, I know you are not an Economist, but given your experience, I just wanted to ask you what an economic plan is?*

Mr. Mills: Hi Jim. Well; a plan, which also includes an economic plan, is *when* the majority of the people head towards the same or a very similar direction.
June 2017

Jim: *...after 28 years now, I guess that definition of a plan by Mr. Mills is still the most solid one.* "

Below are high-level highlights as of July 2017 in core areas that Professionals operating at the global level need to know:

1. Systemic Risk

- Systemic risk remains high given that markets continue to be at all-time highs. Systemic risk is not being factored in across models. Although, the debt component is noted by many, it is not yet being incorporated in full.
- Debt levels across OECD countries continue to be high (i.e., Debt to Equity ratios in OECD countries continue to be at more than 100% level).
- Deleveraging awareness starts to induce new political awakenings. Regardless of reflation initiatives, unconventional calibration models on both Debt and GDP growths' speeds need to be considered in new assessments going forward.
- Credit Default Swaps (CDS) prices are again on watch; given that geopolitical, economic, political and civil unrests increased systemic risks (e.g., North Korea, China, India, US, Ukraine, Russia, Qatar/Gulf Countries, Greece, some African and Middle Eastern countries, NATO, Ukraine, EU, Brazil, Venezuela). South Korea Credit Default Swaps (CDS) prices increased and remain elevated, given geopolitical events in Asia. Greece CDSs remain high given current negotiations with creditors. Greece debt restructuring has been on since 2009; it has been around eight years to date. Qatar CDSs are at the highest level since November 2016, given tensions with Middle Eastern neighboring countries.
- The generalized increase in polarization across the world is becoming a fact in 2017 that is still not captured in financial models; and further, it is impacting politics, public affairs, and markets and reflected in volatility, of

AN OVERVIEW OF WORLD MACRO

which some spikes may appear to be clustered in the future and others may impact at the system level. It is worth noting that polarization impedes the resolution of problems and increases volatility.

- The US Congress is under challenging negotiation schedules (taxes, health care, infrastructure, others) especially given that the US reached the debt ceiling in May 2017. **The debt ceiling is expected to be discussed further in 2017.**
- **The United Kingdom continues negotiations with the European Union on Brexit.**
- Questions, such as **whether Eurozone reform will happen, are beginning to be raised;** along with questioning of the effectiveness of the economic fundamentals in member countries of the EU. Brexit, debt negotiations with some EU countries, and other corporate results, **such as the earnings of the largest EU banks given their latest reported earnings, are likely to add volatility to markets. The EU is mapping out mechanisms in case of bank runs.** This comes after events like the bank-rescue by the Italian Government during mid-2017.
- **Trade definition is taking different types and formats of alliances,** given all countries meetings during the first semester of 2017, and **also including meetings before, during, and after the last G20 meetings. This is now visible in foreign policies in many countries that are adapting to the new realities.**
- **Given all bilateral meetings and agreements in the past three-quarters, a new paradigm of path-dependent bilateral coordination agreements might be the "new normal" on foreign policy.** Notwithstanding, if this materializes further, **traditional multilateral aid and funding channels may be directly influenced by this phenomenon.** As a result, it might **have a direct effect**

on emerging markets and the composition of these types of funding and investments. These are other aspects **that need to be captured in financial and funding models going forward.**

2. Financial Modeling

- Financial Markets expect further rate rises from Central Banks. However, while Central Banks' models and Quantitative Easing (QE) programs face challenges to revive Economies, **they face a bigger challenge to how to unwind their asset holdings built up after the 2008 crisis. Methods, timing, and priorities have not yet been disclosed.**
- The Basel III framework and models assume that debt is risk-free. The quantum of debt in the system determines that interest rates remain very low and that **many banks are finding it very difficult to generate earnings from their "bread and butter" businesses. Fragility in some banks may start to show up.** It is worth noting that **banks in long term recovery mode are particularly vulnerable** in case of a negative market event. **The ratio of revenues-to-debt has become a key metric and allows us to differentiate between a destabilization process and a sustainable path.**
- **Similarly, under Basel III,** ultra-low bond rates **present** big challenges to **the Re/Insurance Solvency 2 framework, especially** on the traditional **insurance and reinsurance business models.** This effect is observed across the board, where the insurance and banking sectors are under pressure to increase dividends and share buyback programs while being challenged to generate sustainable earnings and sales from regular business in order to fund them. **A potential bond** revaluation **at a time when margins are thin could well tip many players into financial distress.** As mentioned in our

AN OVERVIEW OF WORLD MACRO

previous reports, **Property and Casualty (P&C) Insurance margins have been compressed** due to the influx of yield seeking capital into a market with relatively low barriers to entry. 2017 – **Quarter 2 results indicate further margin compression.**

- The near **zero interest policies in place for more than eight years have affected the definition of "Risk-Free rate" while being in practice against the principles of finance.** In effect, this reads as **"the time value of money is currently suspended." Implications remain to be seen especially on how Central Banks will unwind their asset holdings.**
- The main **Central Banks have different views** on interest rates hikes, timing, and **cross border coordination. Coordination is expected to be a key component** of this process. **The velocity of money remains a concern across the world.**
- **OECD underlying growth is still low.** The data have not yet supported the 3% growth expectation. Markets worldwide are following this topic closely.

3. Markets, Asset Classes, Risks & Opportunities

- Most **Sovereign Wealth Funds (SWFs) in 2017 increased their re-allocations towards private debt strategies, mostly in mezzanine debt, distressed debt, and direct lending, and thereafter, in special situations and venture debt strategies.** Europe is now the top targeted region for private debt exposure. Given their long term horizon, **tactical re-allocations may still be under consideration given new developments under current markets' conditions.**
- Again, Equity and Bond markets continue to register all time high prices. Some commentators point out that equities are priced for growth while bonds are priced for deflation. **This is not aligned with principles in**

economic history. Implications of this effect remain to be seen.

- **Volatility (e.g., VIX Index) has been at the lowest values since 1993.** However, **unusual spikes (i.e., larger than other past reactions)** have been observed in events like Brexit and the US elections *vis-à-vis* volatility's mean reverting characteristics.
- Institutional Investors and large financial institutions are still holding Trillions of USDs in cash with a "wait-and-see" approach. This should be noted along with Central Banks asset holdings un-winding plans. To that end, in-depth trade-off assessments by Institutional Investors may provide signals on re-allocations and hedging scenarios.
- **The Foreign Exchange (FX) and Commodities markets continue to show patterns of market uncertainty,** especially in **Gold and the Swiss Franc that are priced at high levels.** The Swiss Franc follows historical patterns related to uncertainty. Re-allocations to EUR are still to be validated as a safe move. USD with volatility, Pound Sterling with short term volatility.
- **Oil is still below the ~USD 60 break-even point**, hurting oil-based economies and companies but also reflecting the depressed outlook for demand. **Although, OPEC and some non-OPEC countries have reached agreements, the Oil price remains low, and supply is still high.**
- The G20, chaired by Germany in 2017, announced that African healthcare and health to the top of the agenda.

4. Balance Sheet - Hedging

- The Debt problem is also affecting the Pension, Insurance, and Reinsurance sectors. Their **balance sheets may suffer a re-classification to short term** liabilities in case of a large shift. They may fall in value in case of further interest rate hikes or under a no cross border coordination scenario. In that case, debt write-downs are likely to happen. **Many balance sheets have high concentrations of overpriced corporate bonds (i.e., high-yield bonds), which are known for their poor liquidity when volatility** ticks up. This scenario is likely to pose serious challenges to these sectors.

- Sovereign bonds generate very little in returns given the low rate environment. **Many balance sheets are unable to generate sufficient margin to justify sustainable businesses. Investment grade bonds price corrections may severely impact Balance Sheets, of which many remain unhedged.**
- Investment firms may shift from a search for yield approach to a protection of capital strategy, where many are starting to consider staying in cash as a suitable option. However, in the case of large and rapid re-allocations, then liquidity, capacity, and asset class re-allocations may be impacted. In the likelihood of such events, those shifts may need to be measured and hedged.

5. Fiduciary Duty - Corporate Governance Risks

- It has been observed in the news that **many Asset Managers are starting to be cautious** with their positions, basing their decisions on market developments and **also showing concerns on the world economy.**
- **Cyber-attacks have become an element of the systemic risk affecting many consumers and businesses. New regulations may need to bear the difficult trade-offs on costs**; i.e. between consumer protection costs, business costs, and new policies on continuity and contingency planning costs; while at the same time, **developing regulations to promote investments with crowd-in effects to boost**

businesses and capacity building, especially for small businesses or entrepreneurs **in a region, within a developed country, or in emerging markets.**

- Regulatory improvements are still delayed. It is worth noting that in the event of a crisis, **in the absence of regulatory changes, there could be an empty period where market monitoring is marked by a regulatory gap.** In such a scenario, **misalignments would likely impact accountability and fiduciary duties. Given that, bail-in/out agreements and processes will need to be redefined.**

"There is enough money and ingenuity in the system to generate growth. The issue is that money is separated from the ingenuity. Indeed, there are limits to what financial engineering can do and the economic world is influenced by our beliefs about it."

We **define groupthink as a process that involves all market participants** who **dynamically** act, react, think, and pause in unison as a herd by **basing their actions on all types of shared knowledge and by prioritizing them within the scope of the average boundaries of a common thinking with different behavioral decision biases.** As such, groupthink is **a dynamic compact that labels contrarian to the average or outliers to those ideas, thoughts, or actions that are rare or labeled as difficult to happen, which indeed are not within the crowd direction.** This process may have had been labeled in the past as market psychology or herd mentality; However, these later are static characteristics. **Groupthink is dynamic, and** perhaps, a silent process that can last decades or more. Further, **it usually adds to both extremes; systemic risks as well as large positive opportunities.** Again, we find that one key differentiation factor is that **groupthink is indeed a dynamic compact, which can behave randomly, especially during fragmented or rare extreme events.** In parallel, **denial is usually reinforced ex-ante by the avoidance of alternative options**, regardless whether they could be good or bad, but **many times that denial responds to** biases and psychological patterns of **fear.**

"The biggest risk in the financial system is psychological."

DEBT LEVELS

"It's about your balance sheet. It doesn't matter what happens as long as you are ready for it."

Focusing on Systemic Risk:

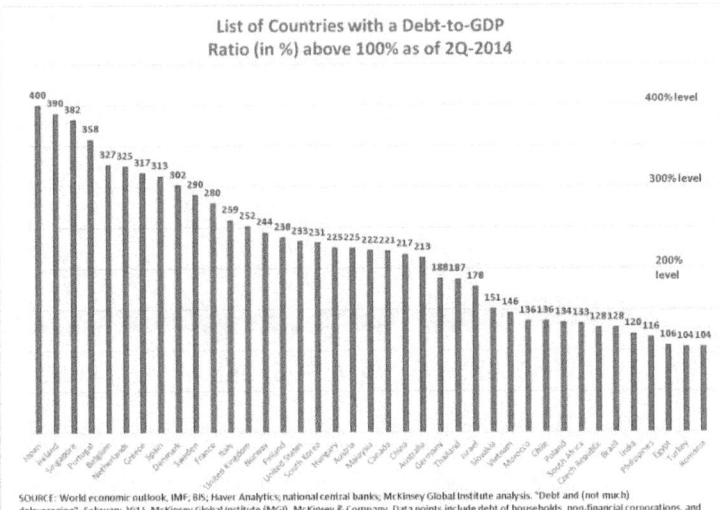

AN OVERVIEW OF WORLD MACRO

- Since 1980, the principal driver of world economic growth has been the growth of debt. In 2016, over USD 6 Trillion in new debt was issued. The impact on economic growth is low.

- The 500 largest companies in the US replaced equity with USD 1 Trillion in debt in 2016, as part of this trend.

- In the years since 2008, over USD 60 Trillion in debt has been issued, while economic growth has managed to total less than USD 20 Trillion.

- Debt has been growing faster than the real economy.

- Debt of all types has seen a surge in market value following the various quantitative easing operations of Central Banks.

- Junk bonds that a couple of years ago yielded 8% now yield 4%. The validity of debt pricing is a serious concern going forward.

- Today, regulatory frameworks such as Solvency 2 and Basel 3 assume that sovereign debt is risk-free. This notion is questionable.

- There are three key constraints to the future issuance of debt:

    1. Debt must be repaid out of real world cash flows.

    2. Debt as an economic stimulant is not as effective as in the past given current debt levels worldwide.

3. Debt sustainability is increasingly challenged. If it is used, cautious management should be considered by also factoring the impact of other drivers at the system level.

Whether or not debt can be managed back to sustainability will be one of the key macroeconomic issues of the next few years.

"...most often people want rapid solutions to issues that have built up for many years. It is like systemic risk; it builds up silently for many years. Therefore, if there are signs of systemic risk or if this is inherited, note that well-thought solutions blended with combinations of tactical fixes apply, esp. if that process was formed over many years. As a basic description, to go from minus ten to zero (or say stabilization) will need phases; and from zero to ten will also require another set of phases. It is not easy, but achievable. As such, solutions are expected to take time, suitable actions, good timing, effective cooperation, and acceptance of trade-offs esp. at the system level."

BLIND SPOTS: BUSINESS-AS-USUAL (BAU) WHEN NOTHING IS AS PER USUAL

"Luck is a matter of preparation meeting opportunity."
- *Lucius Annaeus Seneca*

Recent economic history

How many times have corporate executives told staff that change is permanent? Corporate strategies frequently change in response to business conditions. On a wider timescale, there are economic settings. The last time these changed was in the late 1970s. No economic system ever lasts more than two generations. It seems to be a law of nature.

For years companies have been adding debt to their balance sheets and using leverage to magnify returns. For years debt was used to push growth, both at the company and national level. Governments have been restricting the use of fiscal tools for years. Central Banks have been influencing financial markets by use of one single tool, the interest rate. Capital Market Chartists can tell you how many days the average recession lasted and the typical growth rate of the Standard and Poors 500 in January thanks to the financial stability produced by Central Banks changing the interest rate. Financial Institutions can tell you what the average growth rate has been over the last 30 years and what it will be in the future thanks to the stability provided by Central Banks. Pension funds can invest money knowing that past performance will be repeated in the future. This was an outcome from the stability of the system. We can use the Philips curve to understand likely inflation in the future. In actual fact, so does the Federal Reserve (FED) in its Dynamic Stochastic Generalized Equilibrium model. However, despite significant increases in the money supply, inflation has been very hard to come by.

The reliability of growth

In economics as in sport, the beauty of a stable system is that everyone knows what to expect. Everyone does the same thing because everyone follows the same principles. Some banks will be first movers and make higher profits than regional players, but as long as there is growth, nobody is complaining. Certain consultants can devise new products and sell them to entire industry sectors, knowing that stability guarantees the success of their offerings. There is no need to worry about the big picture because everybody follows Central Banks. Corporate bankers merge companies knowing that savings on staff will lead to growth. Stock market analysts will use the same metrics everyone uses. Like Earning-per-Share (EPS). There is no need to even think about it. As long as earnings are rising why would you use anything else? Buy-side analysts recommend stocks on the basis of their growth potential. The Standard and Poors 500

AN OVERVIEW OF WORLD MACRO

has pushed forward in every decade for more than 40 years. People do not even need to think about it. Occasionally, some weirdo shows up and is instantly labeled as a "contrarian." But for the vast majority of companies, nothing changes. Every major listed company will have set out its goals for 2017+, and all of them will be targeting growth of at around 10% in order to cover their cost of capital and give a bit extra to shareholders. Growth is a given. It is as natural as daybreak. Models' assumptions used to date delivers these outcomes, however, unlike in the past, today's debt levels need to be factored in.

Unavoidable facts

Both Keynes and Galbraith figured out that capitalism is inherently unstable. Further, economist Hyman Minsky noted that there are financing schemes that are stable and financing schemes which are unstable. No Organization for Economic Co-operation and Development (OECD) Central Bank appears able to generate 2% inflation or to generate growth in excess of 2% as originally expected by their models. So, 2% is what one would typically expect given population growth, improvements, and innovation due to technology. However, Central Banks are still facing challenges to generate such growth.

Based on these models, there is no other logic to the system. Without growth, there is no point. The system is breaking down again, just like it did in the 1970s. That time, the problem was unrealistic labor demands. This time the problem is capital. There is simply too much capital clogging up the system. Business-as-usual and the Phillips curve are under pressure. Until this issue is dealt with, growth will be a challenge.

Signs that we are not in business-as-usual:

- The Phillips Curve is not contributing to model growth and detect early signals of tail risks.
- The quantum of debt is very high.
- Sales-to-debt for the Standard and Poors 500.
- Despite an additional USD 6 trillion in global debt last year, economic growth was very low.
- Despite a significant increase in OECD money supply since 2009, there has been no corresponding increase in inflation, as the Central Bank models would expect.
- The FED's growth expectations of 3% are not being met, as originally estimated.
- Political instability in many countries.
- Polarization in societies.
- Payrises are very low, as is the creation of creation of quality jobs.
- The world's 50 largest Fast-moving consumer goods (FMCG) companies are unable to grow sales.
- The US labor participation rates are at mid-1970s levels.
- Investment banks struggle to generate 10% return on equity.
- Oil prices are below breakeven point, impacting the industry and oil-based countries.
- The Swiss Franc (CHF/EUR) exchange rate is signaling flight to safety patterns.
- The gold price remains high.

It is almost ten years into one of the biggest economic crises in history, and models are still delivering these type outcomes. These blind spots in the models used to date could not advise leveling off today's debt levels. These models' business-as-usual outcomes have been enabling the buildup of debt and systemic risk where nothing is as per usual.

MARKET PSYCHOLOGY: MARK-TO-MARKET VERSUS MARK-TO-REALITY

"(Random) Talks:

- *Many conversations about instruments rather than capacity.*
- *Many talks about allocations rather than market-depth.*
- *Many conversations about selection rather than liquidity.*
- *Many talks about assets pricing rather than scenarios of mark-to-new-realities.*
- *Many conversations about growth rather than the dynamic speed(s) of its components."*

Financial markets cannot function without shared understandings of how the economic system works.

Shared understandings deliver the assurance that market participants need. They also provide the intellectual framework of groupthink. However, theories commonly thus far failed to anticipate the 2008 financial crisis or earlier crashes, and are unlikely to spot the next one. These theories faced challenges. How can anything else be possible when the underlying assumption is that markets are in a state of equilibrium that can only be disturbed by unpredictable events unconnected to market operations?

Market crises are generated by the markets, because of how markets operate. Most economists assume that individuals are rational beings making rational choices, but more frequent and larger crises have proved that this is questionable. Markets are human, on a larger scale. They are driven by emotions. When markets fall, the emotion of fear takes over. Markets are thus primarily psychological.

Markets are also prone to herding. Everybody follows everybody else. This is also all too human. Herding drives trends. Trends drive momentum. Momentum draws everyone in with the belief that it is a sure-fire investment. Prior to the 2008 crisis, home-buyers, mortgage lenders, investment banks, rating agencies, and even Central Bankers, all were all drawn into the view that neither the housing bubble nor the explosion of subprime and Alt-A lending was a particular threat. Different risk management frameworks and models from audit firms, bank risk committees, rating agencies, regulators and Central Banks, should have capture signals warning about the risks materialized in 2008, but did not. It is hard to stop the herd especially when they react based on the use of models that are not updated to capture systemic risk signs.

AN OVERVIEW OF WORLD MACRO

Groupthink is a particular problem with herding. The longer one spends observing the world from a particular frame of reference the more difficult it can be to accept an alternative point of view. The financial services industry has two groupthink strengthening influences. The more of their career and reputation someone has invested in a particular frame of reference, the harder it is for them to accept evidence that undermines it. When evidence in contradiction of their worldview emerges, it will most likely be ignored. The second relates to the power of incentive – when people are paid large amounts of money to pursue a particular set of objectives. Under this framework, those people defend the integrity of those objectives, and it is expected that they are going to question the validity of any frame of reference that challenges those objectives.

The **shared understandings** of the market work well until they no longer work and security prices fall, suddenly. It can perhaps be understood as akin to charting the payoff diagram of a binary option (i.e., with zero or one as outcomes). There is nothing rational about this. As in 2008, the recognition of the scale of financial model miscalculations creates a rush for liquidity, causing huge losses, triggering margin calls and downgrades that cause more selling, damage confidence, and further squeeze credit. That is the paradox of deleveraging. One firm can, but the system as a whole cannot.

One of the big lessons from 2008 was that no one in the financial system understood either the extent of the vast risks that were being accumulated or where those risks lay. Today, similar models are still being used. Our worldwide connected financial system spreads miscalculations of risk management from one institution to another via groupthink and the balance sheet assets.

Consequently, another major problem with markets and their models is that they are unable to price tail risk. One of the reasons for this is that herds need very simple instructions or shared understandings to move forward. In the case of markets, the driver is the desire for profit. And when the profit has all been squeezed out, it is very hard for the herd to retreat rationally or to adjust safely to the new reality. In times of large scale crises, vulnerable members of the herd are picked off by predators. A summary of the 2008 crisis follows:

- In late 2008, most forms of funding left the financial system. This process dried up liquidity in key financial markets and strained banks' balance sheets because of plummeting asset values and hard to roll over liabilities. The system was simply not ready for such a dramatic turnaround in correlations, triggering all sorts of amplification mechanisms, ranging from tightening in margin requirements to a sudden rise in uncertainty.

- In real life, unlike in many models, crises are not an instant but operate over time. This time dimension creates an opportunity for all sorts of strategic decisions within a crisis. Weaker players must decide when and if to let go of their assets, knowing that a miscalculation on the right timing can be very costly. Speculators and strategic players have to decide when to reinforce a downward spiral, and when to stabilize it. Governments have to decide how long to wait before intervening. All have consequences and difficult trade-offs.

- In deregulated financial systems, crises are inevitable, like earthquakes on a fault zone. Only the timing is uncertain. Galbraith and Keynes both focused on the instability of modern capitalism in terms of the drive to accumulate excessive wealth and the fragile nature of the financial system. A further problem is the

AN OVERVIEW OF WORLD MACRO

    refusal of key players to study simple history or the history of capitalism.

- Once crisis strikes, mark-to-market becomes a problem, especially when there is little or no market for many securities. In 2008, there was a widespread view, given the paucity of transactions that prices were at fire sale levels, not true values.

- The Mark-to-market approach, therefore, works well for business-as-usual conditions, but is unsuitable for periods of market stress, either on the upside during times of exuberance or the downside during periods of deleveraging. The financial system is essentially psychological rather than rational. It is prone to instability and unable to price tail risk. As such, models are biased by "groupthink comfortable frameworks driven by accepted drivers" that lose groundings to detect the buildup of systemic risks ex-ante. This happens both for the transition, to periods of instability, and during periods of instability.

- **Mark-to-market becomes mark-to-reality, overnight.**

IS THE TIME VALUE OF MONEY SUSPENDED? YIELD CURVES, INTEREST RATES POLICIES, SOLVENCY 2

"...it couldn't happen here."

Is the Time Value of Money suspended? Yield Curves, Interest Rates Policies, Solvency 2.

Just use any yield curve over 20 years as a picture. **The relation between what we see and what we know is never settled.**

Yield curves are a feature of financial markets. They are called curves because yields tend to increase over time, given that a bird in the hand is worth 2 in the bush. **They are not

AN OVERVIEW OF WORLD MACRO

lines. As a random example, Dutch life insurance is a backwater of the global financial system, but it is nonetheless exposed to many of the features of the system in 2017. The Netherlands is one of the "strong" countries of the Eurozone with a reputation for level headedness and seriousness when it comes to money. Its bonds are very much in demand, consequently, to the point where sovereign bonds at various durations have yields around or below zero.

A bond with a negative yield delivers a negative return. This goes against all of the basic principles of finance. The world of crypto-currencies such as Bitcoin has a test for the validity of a scheme, **known as the Howey Test. The requirement is that an investment of money is accompanied by a "reasonable expectation of profits." This is in line with the natural order of things.** Trees do it. Fleas do it. Money used to do it.

How does the phenomenon of negative yields work in practice?

Continuing with the example, a Dutch insurance company has a portfolio of medium term business. Cash flows extend for 20 years. The company is regulated under Europe's **Solvency 2 system. Solvency 2 is based on the idea that insurance companies must be market consistent. They must follow the logic of the yield curves of the financial markets, for better or worse.**
The **long term average yield** expected by the Insurance Supervisors of Europe **is 4.2%. This is composed of 2.2% to represent the long term average real rate and 2%, which is the ECB's target rate of inflation.**

In 2011, The European Central Bank (ECB) launched its **Quantitative Easing (QE) program,** flooding the market with money **in a bid to reach its inflation target of**

2%. Instead, something very unusual happened. Bond yields fell well below 2%, including in the Netherlands.

In year 1 of its projection, the **insurance company follows the market** with a yield of minus 0.172% (- 0.172%). The yield turns positive in year 4 with 0.007%. Yields rise very slowly to 1.247% in year 20. **Given the negative yields in the early years, the net value** of a sum of 100 invested at time zero (T0) would be 100 by time 6 (T6), **i.e., no change whatsoever.**

There are several problems with this approach:

1. The **regular calculation of yield curves does not appear to work** at very low yields.

2. An approach that **has a yield at every duration below the long term average does not appear to be coherent.**

3. **Neither does the idea that low yields can be maintained for very long durations.** Otherwise, how did the average of a 4.2 mark happen?

4. **The validity of the market yield curve is also questionable.** Why are rates so low? Does it make sense that they would increase again in the absence of a resolution of the problem that led to the decrease in the first place? **Why would rates increase if the problem that led to near zero yields has not been addressed further?**

There is a huge question mark over the validity of market yield curves in the third quarter of 2017. **Markets take things as they come, without much thinking. It is not possible for herds to consider developments deeply.** The normal approach for yield curve is an increasing trend, in part to reflect the time value of money. But many yields at shorter duration are negative, in which case the time value of money is suspended. **Building a regular yield curve assumes that the time value of money will be switched on at some point. Without questioning why this is the case**; or when it is likely to happen, or why it is impossible to verify the market yield curve.

Financial markets have at least three key features:

- They tend to **operate in herds** *and run* **groupthink**

- They **follow trends**.

- **They cannot price tail risk.**

It is easy to follow a trend without thinking about it. The trend doesn't necessarily need to be rational. Markets can follow trends; however, they are not good at anticipating trend reversals. Further, they have weaknesses at predicting shocks or large scale volatility events.

Economic history is not linear. Ultra-low-interest rates are a symptom of several problems at the system level.

Bond prices are too high. **Discretion is required.**

WORLD POLARIZATION SNAPSHOT AS OF JULY 2017

Polarization as a systemic risk is observed in the aftermath of serious economic crashes. Voters become more ideologically polarized in the aftermath of banking, debt, or inflation crises leading to a breakdown in the normal political "business as usual," a fall in support for traditional parties and a rise in polarization, as loss allocation is carried out. Government coalitions become weaker in terms of both vote shares and seat shares. **It becomes harder for Governments to retain power. Opposition coalitions become larger.**

Inequality is a key driver of polarization, while both add up to more systemic risk. The allocation of losses in societies post crisis tends to disfavor certain groups, with a consequent increase in the level of political frustration. **Inequality may be one of many drivers of polarization in some countries or the main one in others. A phenomenon can be seen across economic dislocations reaching back to the 1850s.**

AN OVERVIEW OF WORLD MACRO

The chart below summarizes the results of elections or voting referendums in a sample of countries where the divide in societies can be observed. **In addition to these results, there are other countries, for example, Brazil and Venezuela, with high political instability, and others like Spain and Greece, with high unemployment and low growth rates.**

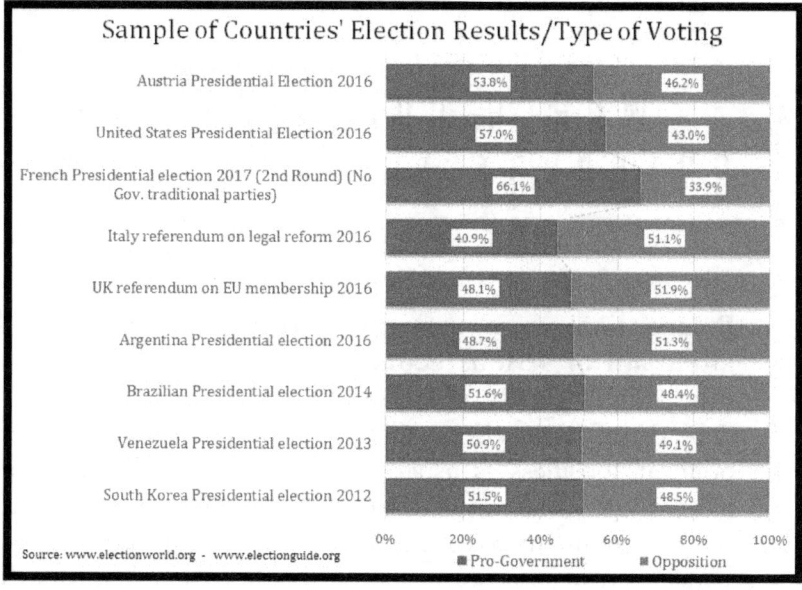

The period since 2008 has been marked by increased levels of polarization across many OECD countries. It has also been seen across core and peripheral economies in recent years. In the world system, polarization in core economies is ultimately replicated in peripheral economies. Examples follow:

- In France with the Front Nationale making it to the second round of the 2017 Presidential election.

- Ongoing political instability in Italy including the removal of the Prime Minister by the Eurozone (2011).

- In the UK following the Brexit vote.

- In the US with the 2016 election.

- In Greece and Spain due to high levels of unemployment.

- In the rise of right politicians in the Netherlands, France, and Austria (2016).

- The political landscape in Turkey (2016).

- Political instability in Venezuela, Egypt, and Ukraine (ongoing).

- Impeachments in South Korea and Brazil; and a divided society in Argentina.

Polarization typically manifests itself in terms of a disconnect between the mainstream of society and its politicians, who are no longer able to address political needs within their business as usual frameworks. Polarization widens the differences between the policy programs of opposing parties or opposing groups within governments, resulting in policy jolts when circumstances change.

Levels of trust break down. Political cooperation is reduced. These translate into political programs that are likely to become challenged by the public. **Governments as they get elected, they must consider important issues** like the lack of political cooperation or the lack of resources, while being observed **by the voters and markets may shift**

gear by expecting and timing developments. These issues are drivers of systemic risk.

Financial markets find it very difficult to price these political developments. For instance, most market players assumed that the remaining side would win the 2016 Brexit vote and drove the price of sterling up to USD 1.50, for example. It subsequently fell in short order to $1.25. The trade following the US election hit US treasury yields out on the expectation of growth and inflation last November of 2016. It has since deflated.

Polarization reduces the likelihood of reform. Divided societies typically find it difficult to find a way out of the situation. This becomes a vicious circle. From a risk point of view, polarization is a serious threat to stability. **Structural risks remain** *in situ* **and are not dealt with.** Political instability can deliver decisions that could hurt cash flow assumptions. **Polarization increases the exposure to the unknown that is something that translates into uncertainty or anything that is not known, which markets price rapidly.**

Disconnects build up gradually over time. Regardless of any political affiliations, political swings or economic views, what we now see consistently across the world is the accumulation of many issues not being addressed over time, which together constitute a clear and present significant problem. Markets and economies work best when companies, governments, and the people share similar direction and values. Without this, stability is difficult to achieve.

The major challenge for governments and economic policy makers is to engage with the key issues while there is still time; before systemic risk becomes unmanageable.

IS BREXIT AN ECONOMIC OR A GEOPOLITICAL MOVE?

The vote to leave the European Union was unexpected to win and is an evidence of a "business-as-usual" (BAU) and groupthink.

There tend to be two framings of Brexit: one geopolitical and the other economic. Short run readings point to economic implications. Long term analysis may not. Currently, the UK economy is facing some challenges. Many of these affect the Brexit vote. More specifically on the economy, the previous administration promised to get the UK's budget deficit down to zero by the time of the 2015 election. The model was built in the effect of austerity cuts, and pay rises to see how long it would take to get the deficit back to zero. The key assumption was the rate of payrises. If Government spending is cut, then the private sector needs to respond in order to keep things moving.

AN OVERVIEW OF WORLD MACRO

Payrolls have not had increases in excess of inflation for a long time. This did not change while the deficit target plan was in place and cuts were implemented to programs. The deficit remained high due to structural issues. The private sector continued keeping payrolls down. Prior to 2014, the UK had a manageable GDP growth rate compared to other economies in the EU, such as France and Italy. Corporate profits remain high. In essence, the economic situation can be summarized by analyzing the following five factors:

1. **Productivity**

Productivity is one of the main drivers of economic growth, but it is still stagnant in the UK. Growth happens when companies invest in their businesses and people and drive productivity increases, which result in pay rises that are used to drive spending. Poor productivity is also a factor of management incentives. Instead of investing in their own business, companies are incentivized by bonuses and shares buybacks. Business investments are very low, while profit margins are high. This follows a short term fashion.

There are currently ongoing problems with the three main drivers of UK productivity businesses (oil, finance, and utilities). Oil has been a large component of economic activity over the past 40 years and had relatively low numbers of workers as a portion of the output, with productivity improvements prominent. Finance had been the main driver of UK growth in the run up to 2008 and very innovative. These three sectors productive represent around 20 % of UK gross domestic product (GDP). Productivity was ultimately one of the main reasons why the deficit was not closed. As a reference, the estimate in October 2016 was that there would be a 40% chance of the UK having a deficit of zero by 2020.The 2016 Autumn Statement revealed that the UK government had abandoned guidance on a date by when the deficit would be reduced to zero.

2. Monetary policy

In 2014, the Bank of England (BoE) imposed a high-level target as they confirmed to return inflation to target in a two-year horizon. This target became a challenge to be accomplished.

3. The labor market

According to Craig Holmes, who is an academic at Oxford and a research associate at the Centre on Skills, Knowledge and Organizational Performance, "In the replacement of those middle-level jobs, the UK has shifted far more towards lower-skilled service work than lots of other European countries…." Subsidizing low wage employment through tax credits encourages low wage, low skill businesses, and therefore, low skill workers. This explains somehow the UK's performance on employment, its relatively higher growth rate before 2015 although not on a per capita basis. The long-term pattern of jobs growth in the UK, as in most other European countries, has been stark - the share of mid-skilled jobs has been squeezed, while the share of low-skilled jobs and high-skilled jobs have expanded. In the corporate sector, investment/consumption growth in the UK will have to come from wage increases rather than from falling savings ratios.

4. Economic growth

This has been driven by population growth rather than productivity and payrises. British households remain heavily indebted, not least because they have not seen wages increase in real terms (i.e., nominal wages over inflation rates). The

AN OVERVIEW OF WORLD MACRO

fact that deficit targets were missed due to wage deflation, with very low productivity growth led to low salary growth.

5. Trade deficit

Despite a 25% real depreciation of Pound Sterling in 2007-08, the current account deficit deteriorated to end 2015 at 5.2% of the GDP, one of the largest in British history, leaving the UK economy in a weak status. On December 1, 2014, an article in the Financial Times stated:

"But, from here, it would be rare for the private sector to shift substantially into financial deficit by increasing its expenditure further relative to income. Growth in private activity will, therefore, need to come from a rise in income, especially wages, not from falling savings ratios. That will be a more difficult process, especially if fiscal policy is being tightened at the same time. The second phase of the fiscal correction may, therefore, be even harder to attain than the first. A simultaneous contraction in both fiscal and monetary policy looks problematic: something will surely have to give." Source: Gavyn Davies, Financial Times. December 1, 2014.

The key points about Brexit can be summarized as follows:

- Brexit will face trade-offs, to be assessed as the exit progresses with a forward looking approach, including encompassing a geopolitical view.

- The UK will be tested on being able to deliver what Leave voters expect.

- No help is likely to be made available by France or Germany.

- Cost assessments need to factor in geopolitics, as a series of trade-offs as the Leave actions move forward.

The exit of the UK from the European Union is now a fact, and only time will tell what will weigh the most: a) economics in the short or medium term, b) geopolitics in the long run, or, c) a combination of both.

OIL PRICES IN A NUTSHELL

Overview (May 2017):

Oil prices fell from an average USD90-100/barrel (January to June 2014) to around USD50 a barrel in May of 2017. This decline was mainly fostered by the Organization of the Petroleum Exporting Countries (OPEC) decision (November 2014) to maintain the production ceiling at 30 million barrels daily; leaving the production level unchanged as it was maintained since 2011. In May 2017, the OPEC decided to cut production levels, but still, the market price remained low. Below are two basic approaches (financial/market and geopolitical) that provide a quick summary overview of the current oil markets. It is worth noting that whatever approach taken, a sustained drop in oil prices may have economic and financial implications on the economies of OPEC´s members and non-members countries, leaving the door open to potential armed conflicts. As a reference, the following chart provides a quick historical retrospective review that summarizes the market and geopolitical events occurred as a result of changes in oil prices in 155 years, from 1861 to 2016.

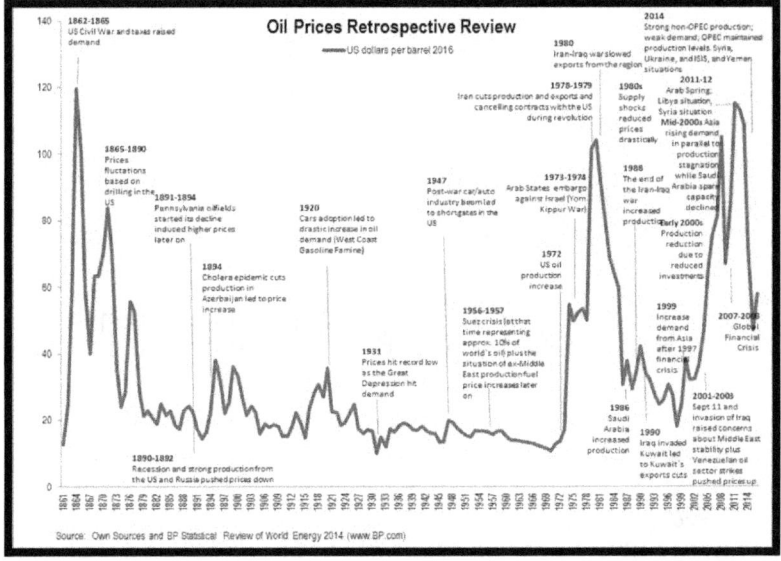

A QUESTION OF SPEED?

"1990s:
Tony: *What's the status, Ben?*
Ben: *It's 4 deviations down, Tony.*
Tony: *They will blame us. I should resign.*
Ben: *Just stay put Tony. We have to go through this.* **It** *should come by now."*

A few (random) facts:

- World markets are at all-time highs.

- Debt levels are high (sovereign, corporate, and household).

- Deb-to-GDP ratios in many countries, especially in most developed countries, are over 100%.

- Total debt issuance has been increasing at high speed since the 2008 crisis.

- In some countries, which are not few, the debt level is leading them to unmanageable scenarios, when the way back to equilibrium is becoming a big challenge unless they undertake difficult decisions and unpopular trade-offs.

- Many models are not yet capturing critical drivers such as polarized societies that add up to systemic risk.

- Corporate revenues have been decreasing for years now along with a decreasing demand.

- The speed of debt growth worldwide has been greater than the speed of demand or the speed of GDP growth. Further, they seemed to have negative correlations (i.e., while debt speed increases, demand and GDP growth speeds decrease).

- Zero interest-rate policy (ZIRP) initiatives boosted the effects of the facts above. Negative interest rates have affected the concept of net present value and have also impacted the effectiveness and notion of the time value of money.

- Solvency discussions have not been embraced in full, mostly based on the use of models that are still not capturing the silent formation of systemic risk. The same has happened with debt levels.

As mentioned above, speed, as a driver, is becoming a big risk today, other things held constant. Indeed, **the speed of debt growth has been higher than the speed of the GDP growth.** As a parallel illustration using options

AN OVERVIEW OF WORLD MACRO

trading analogy, it can be said that the "delta" of debt has been higher than the "delta" of GDPs. Given this illustration, any trader could formulate trading strategies under this scenario, which has held true for many years to date.

"Hey buddy, we need to lift the dead body. "

Given the above, **there could be many approaches towards solving this (facts-based) equation,** of which **many would be unconventional** like for instance the one that follows below. Note that this is only one of the many approaches or ways that could work. **Combinations and permutations are very useful** in mathematics, which **create innovative ways to partition a problem and combine parts and portions to form solutions to difficult problems.** Sometimes, those proposed solutions are neither perfect nor long-term fixes, **but they may be optimal, suitable, and effective if constructed under phases;** as like in math the partitioning of a problem could lead to the solution to it. *One (of the many) random thought(s) follows:*

Suppose that People in a Jurisdiction **agree in unity to stabilize their no-growth situation** and to keep its GDP growing faster than its Debt, but in phases; let's say in 6 phases as follows:

1. The Government (as a market-maker) re-boost infrastructure (let's say by using a Keynesian approach). Why? Because under a no-growth scenario and given that other monetary tools could not deliver more growth, then it could be faster to intervene (for the moment) to lift infrastructure and industries with the government support.

2. This will most likely increase the crowd-in effect in the private sector and an increase in demand. The process may start slowly while keeping investing in infrastructure and industry. If considering a sectoral approach with different investment speeds that would refine the outcome. In such scenario, calibration, as things move along, is key.

3. Once demand kicks off and growth resumes, then it would be time for the Government to start to phase out and shift more towards a "monitoring role" (let's say to take a more Austrian economic approach), like a "market-maker" would do it: it pushes forward in full at first and then it starts "deleveraging" its market share, leaving the private sector operating under their "monitoring role" at the end.

4. The velocity of money (and speed of growth/demand) may increase further. Given that not all sectors are able to ride along well yet, government intervention as "market-maker" can develop those other under-served sectors (again, let's say with Keynesian economic approach), while at the same time reducing regulations in other developed sectors, including the financial sector (now let's say: taking an Austrian economics approach). The government acts as a "market-maker" does, by phasing out from its first push-investor-role to phase into a "monitoring role" (i.e., it uses a mix of tools from the Austrian and Keynesian economics approaches). The private sector crowd in effect takes place. Again, sectoral prioritization and targeting would be a fundamental decision as trade-offs increase or diminish (to be discovered).

5. As the velocity of growth and demand accelerates, the velocity of debt would follow; but also, the velocity of money would follow as well, but now, cash flows would

AN OVERVIEW OF WORLD MACRO

come from other sources (revenues, payraises, etc.). Although, debt level is high and becomes higher, these actions may reactivate the "heavy-machinery" and the speed of GDP growth. Other sectors, and especially the financial sector, would follow.

6. In all these phases, the "economy" is managed unconventionally, like "a car," where interest rate decisions are used as both a "speedometer" and a "calibrator"; in some cases to boost some sectors and in other cases to phase out from others. The same applies for fiscal policies. In addition, the economy may face times of inflation and in other cases times of no-inflation and also sometimes like "with a peg." The most important take away is the notion of "flexibility" of using tools rather than defending a theory. If these phases are achieved, then stabilization would come faster.

One approach that is critical is to start by thinking in reverse, or like a kind of reverse engineering ("setting few goals and using all suitable and needed tools available in the economic theories toolbox to achieve them").

Today, one big issue is to increase growth, or like in the option illustration, to increase its delta. The use of theories as tools and dynamically (blending economic tools from different economic theories) is something to consider as a viable option, given that **history has proved that using only one of them may have worked in the past when current economic and financial drivers were not so risky as they are today. Today the landscape has changed.** Adapting those tools and devising the best suitable timing for each phase may provide results faster, which so far they were not achieved with current models and stand-alone theories.

Sometimes, the biggest risk is psychological. Many risks are also based on Egos and Fear. *Perhaps today, it is all about "suitability," "timing," "coordination," "alignment," and "speed."* And **perhaps, it is about time to think about that toolbox as a suitable option**, which by the way, they may have the same traditional tools, **but just applied unconventionally.**

*"We'd better run ... or they will start **criticizing** us!"*

Taking a high-level view, many models and frameworks have been built and continually refined on the basis of "blaming others" and not on the basis of "Fairness to focus on solving the issue at hand." The *result* of this effect *can be seen in today markets' behaviors, divided societies, increased polarization, geopolitical events, uncoordinated moves, and the comfortable belief and complacency that crises will not happen again; when they are becoming much more frequent and more profound.* **This can be read as a denial of many risks by believing that they will fade away fast. Complexities fortified those models and frameworks' basis, solidifying those perspectives.**

Furthermore, many models have been framed for years based on the idea to foster "who is right" and "who is wrong"; rather than "what is right" or "what needs to be done." *Most of the models and frameworks have backed the idea that they can explain nonlinear complexities by using their linear basis* **when the world operates in a non-linear way.** As a result, outputs and outcomes of ***those models have advised decision makers for years by providing them with incomplete information.*** This is a nonlinear way to **call for an upgrade** of those models, while at the same time keeping their best tools and creating **new unconventional and complementary alternatives.**

... just another random thought.

CONCLUSION

This book has provided the audience with an **overview of the critical fundamentals on World-Macro to protect your balance sheet at a critical time**.

This book gives **Investors, Chairmen, Chief Executive Officers, Chief Investment Officers, Chief Risk Management Officers, Board Members** in our audience to have a MUCH clearer understanding of the mistakes with **systemic risk, financial modeling, investment opportunities, balance sheet hedging, fiduciary duty** - and how to avoid them today.

We thank YOU all for claiming the copy of for our book about **World-Macro** and the REAL truth about how to protect their balance sheets at a critical time and **in order to fulfill the fiduciary duty.**

Have a great day!

www.DirectionalAlpha.com

DISCLAIMER

This material or content is intended to provide general information on the subject, especially on systemic risk, tail risk, volatility, investment, finance, financial modeling only. Neither the author nor publisher provides any legal or other professional advice. If you need professional advice, you should seek advice from the appropriate licensed professional. This report or content does not provide complete information on the subject matter covered. This report is not intended to address specific requirements, either for an individual or an organization. This report or content is intended to be used only as a general guide, and not as a sole source of information on the subject matter. While the author has undertaken diligent efforts to ensure accuracy, there is no guarantee of accuracy or no errors, omissions or typographical errors. Any slights of people or organizations are unintentional. Any reference to any person or organization whether living or dead is purely coincidental. The author and publisher shall have no liability or responsibility to any person or entity and hereby disclaim all liability, including without limitation, liability for consequential damages regarding any claim, loss or damage that may be incurred, or alleged to have been incurred, directly or indirectly, arising out of the information provided in this report. No part of this material or content may be used, reproduced, distributed or transmitted in any form and by any means whatsoever, including without limitation photocopying, recording or other electronic or mechanical methods or by any information storage and retrieval system, without the prior written permission of the author, except for brief excerpts in a review.

Use of this content, Directional Alpha, LLC or the www.DirectionalAlpha.com website, and related sites and applications is provided under the www.DirectionalAlpha.com Terms of Use and other Disclaimers posted at www.DirectionalAlpha.com. The information provided in this publication is private, privileged, and confidential information, licensed for your sole individual use as a subscriber and/or purchaser. Directional Alpha, LLC reserves all rights to the content of this publication and

AN OVERVIEW OF WORLD MACRO

related materials. Forwarding, copying, disseminating, or distributing this report in whole or in part, including substantial quotation of any portion the publication or any release of specific investment recommendations, is strictly prohibited. Participation in such activity is grounds for immediate termination of all subscriptions of registered subscribers deemed to be involved at Directional Alpha, LLC's sole discretion, may violate the copyright laws of the United States of America, and may subject the violator to legal prosecution. Directional Alpha, LLC reserves the right to monitor the use of this publication without disclosure by any electronic means it deems necessary and may change those means without notice at any time. If you have received this publication and are not the intended subscriber or purchaser, please contact us by filling out the contact form located in the contact sections of Directional Alpha, LLC's website: www.DirectionalAlpha.com. Directional Alpha, LLC reserves the right to cancel any subscription at any time, and if it does so, it will promptly refund to the subscriber the amount of the subscription payment previously received relating to the remaining subscription period. Cancellation of a subscription may result from any unauthorized use or reproduction or rebroadcast of any Directional Alpha, LLC publication or website, any infringement or misappropriation of Directional Alpha, LLC's proprietary rights, or any other reason determined in the sole discretion of Directional Alpha,

www.DirectionalAlpha.com LLC.

This book/report represents an opinion of the authors based on their analysis on the subject. This should be taken and considered for illustrative or educational purpose, which is subject to changes. As such, the reader should consider that it is subject to changes both at present and in the future. The Directional Alpha, LLC website (www.DirectionalAlpha.com), the 360 Pagers or 360 Series, Article Postings, and Blog Postings are published by Directional Alpha, LLC. The information contained in such publications is obtained from sources believed to be reliable, but its accuracy cannot be guaranteed. The information contained in such publications is not intended to constitute individual investment advice and is not designed to meet your personal financial situation. The opinions expressed in such publications are those of the publisher and are subject to change without notice. The information in such publications may become outdated, and there is no obligation to update any such information. You are advised to discuss with your financial advisers your investment options and whether any investment is suitable for your specific needs prior to making any investments. Further, the analysis and materials contained herein are for informational purposes only and do not constitute legal, financial, tax, accounting or investment advice. The studies and analysis conducted in this document

AN OVERVIEW OF WORLD MACRO

were constructed for illustrative purposes on the basis of knowledge, models, and sources generally accepted by the market practitioners. Its results may differ from the developments of markets, corporate, economic and/or political events at present and/or in the future. Any action and/or decision of any kind based on the use of the information contained in this document are under the sole and only responsibility of the reader/user of this document. The information contained herein is provided "as is" without any express or implied guarantee. The authors of this report or content neither are nor will be liable for damages and/or financial and/or economic direct, indirect, special, consequential, punitive or incidental damages, monetary losses and/or arising and/or related to the use or unauthorized use of the findings, conclusions, and material contained in this report.

Investing is Inherently Risky: there are risks inherent in all investments, which may make such investments unsuitable for certain persons. These include, for example, economic, political, currency exchange, rate fluctuations, and limited availability of information on international securities. You may lose all of your money on trading and investing. Past performance of an investment is not necessarily indicative of its future results. No assurance can be given that any investment will be profitable or will not be subject to losses. Hypothetical results are reported: results and examples used in the Directional Alpha, LLC's advertisements, books, videos, websites, and other media are, in some cases, based on hypothetical (simulated) financial models and trading models. Hypothetical performance results have certain limitations. Unlike an actual performance record, hypothetical results do not represent actual trading. Hypothetical financial models generally are also subject to the fact that they are designed with the benefit of hindsight. Hypothetical results also do not account for commissions or slippage or different pricing and outcomes.

Information provided by Directional Alpha, LLC is not investment advice. Directional Alpha, LLC is not a registered investment adviser, stock broker, or brokerage. You agree that the Directional Alpha, LLC does not represent, warrant, or take responsibility that any account will or is likely to achieve profit or losses similar to those shown. Examples published by Directional Alpha, LLC are selected for illustrative purposes only. No independent party has audited any hypothetical performance contained in this report, nor has any independent party undertaken to confirm that they reflect the model under the assumptions or conditions specified. Offers disinterested commentary and analysis: Offers disinterested commentary and analysis: Directional

AN OVERVIEW OF WORLD MACRO

Alpha, LLC does not receive any form of payment or other compensation for publishing information, news, research, or any other material concerning specific securities on the network that is intended to affect or influence the value of securities.

Directional Alpha, LLC and other entities in which he has an interest, employees, officers, family, and associates may from time to time have positions in the securities or commodities covered in this report or its website. Directional Alpha, LLC and its management may benefit from an increase or decrease in the share prices of the profiled companies or economic scenarios in any markets. If a particular security featured in a newsletter, report, or publication is concurrently owned by Directional Alpha, LLC in its corporate brokerage account, or in any of the individual accounts of the Directional Alpha, LLC's staff, that fact will be disclosed. Directional Alpha, LLC and its Staff may choose to purchase a security or derivative featured in one of its newsletter publications but typically will wait 3 (three) trading days from the date of publication before initiating said purchase. Company policies are in effect that attempts to avoid potential conflicts of interest and resolve conflicts of interest that do arise in a timely fashion. By using Directional Alpha, LLC's reports and its website and other services provided, you agree not to hold Directional Alpha, LLC, or any of its affiliates, liable for decisions that are based on information contained in blog posts, reader responses to blog posts, or information anywhere else on their website or in promotional material.

By using Directional Alpha, LLC's report, and/or content, and/or analyses, and/or website you agree to the Terms of Use, the Privacy Policy, and other Disclaimers posted at Directional Alpha, LLC's website (www.DirectionalAlpha.com). You also agree and accept that these Terms of Use and other Disclaimers will be updated regularly and it is your responsibility to review all updates frequently and on a regular basis by visiting Directional Alpha, LLC website at www.DirectionalAlpha.com.

Copyright © 2017 Directional Alpha, LLC. All rights reserved worldwide.

www.ingramcontent.com/pod-product-compliance
Lightning Source LLC
Chambersburg PA
CBHW050239230526
45470CB00005B/2021